# ELECTRIC ANIMALS

# SHARKS
## SENSE ELECTRICITY!

BY LOUIS MALLORY

Gareth Stevens
PUBLISHING

Please visit our website, www.garethstevens.com. For a free color catalog of all our high-quality books, call toll free 1-800-542-2595 or fax 1-877-542-2596.

**Cataloging-in-Publication Data**
Names: Mallory, Louis.
Title: Sharks sense electricity! / Louis Mallory.
Description: New York : Gareth Stevens Publishing, 2024. | Series: Electric animals | Includes glossary and index.
Identifiers: ISBN 9781538293027 (pbk.) | ISBN 9781538293034 (library bound) | ISBN 9781538293041 (ebook)
Subjects: LCSH: Sharks–Juvenile literature. | Electric fishes–Juvenile literature.
Classification: LCC QL638.9 M355 2024 | DDC 597.3–dc23

Published in 2024 by
**Gareth Stevens Publishing**
2544 Clinton Street
Buffalo, NY 14224

Designer: Claire Wrazin
Editor: Natalie Humphrey

Photo credits: Cover, p. 1 Ramon Carretero/Shutterstock.com; background (series art) Romashka2/Shutterstock.com; p. 5 Lewis Burnett/Shutterstock.com; p. 7 (top) Dudarev Mikhail/Shutterstock.com, (inset) wildestanimal/Shutterstock.com, (bottom) LuckyStep/ Shutterstock.com; p. 9 Yann hubert/Shutterstock.com; p. 11 Mohamed Shareef/ Shutterstock.com; p. 13 Joern_k/Shutterstock.com; p. 15 VisionDive/Shutterstock.com; p. 17 Natursports/Shutterstock.com; p. 19 Sergey Uryadnikov/Shutterstock.com; p. 21 Tomas Kotouc/Shutterstock.com.

Printed in the United States of America

CPSIA compliance information: Batch #CW24GS: For further information contact Gareth Stevens, New York, New York at 1-800-542-2595.

Find us on

# CONTENTS

**Boldface** words appear in the glossary.

## Top Hunters

Sharks are top predators in their ocean homes. But it isn't just their powerful **jaws** and sharp teeth that make them deadly. Sharks can sense **electricity**! This deadly hunter can hunt down their dinner nearly anywhere in the ocean.

## Shark Bodies

There are many kinds of sharks. While they all look a little bit different, they have some things in common. Sharks don't have **scales** like other fish. They have rough, or not smooth, skin instead. They also have many rows of teeth that some use to bite down on their dinner!

**BLACKTIP REEF SHARK**

**GREAT WHITE SHARK**

**SHORT FIN MAKO SHARK**

7

## Sensing Electricity

A shark has special **receptors** they use to sense electricity. Electrical receptors are in the shark's nose, jaws, and head. The receptors are inside small holes on the shark's face and look like small, black dots.

## How Do They Work?

How do the electrical receptors work? When a fish is swimming, its **muscles** make a small amount of electricity. This electricity makes an **electrical field** around the fish. The shark's receptors can sense the field when the fish is close by.

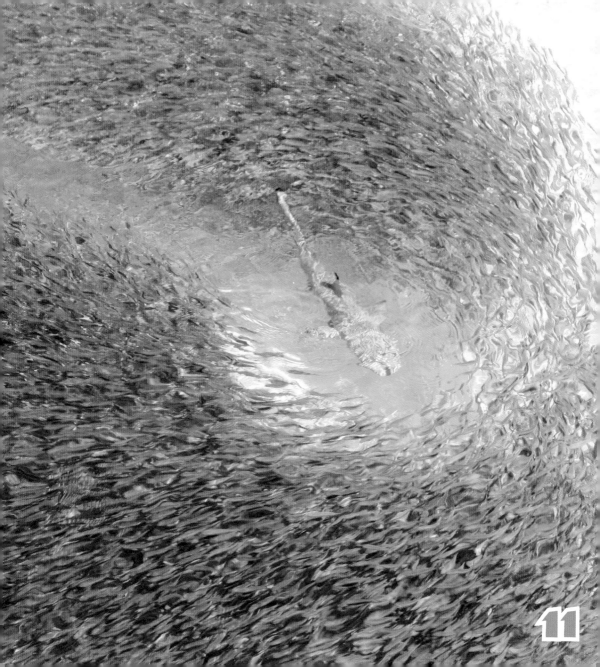

## Sensitive Sharks

Different kinds of sharks use their receptors in different ways. Smaller sharks, such as dogfish, can sense movement from animals hidden in the sand. A baby bonnethead shark is so **sensitive**, it could sense a flashlight battery 10,000 miles (16,000 km) away.

## Tough to Study

Sharks such as great white sharks can use their receptors to find seals miles away. Scientists believe hammerhead sharks may have **evolved** to have wider heads to fit more receptors! But it's very hard for scientists to study these large sharks to know for sure.

## Hunting Without Seeing

When some sharks hunt, they **protect** their eyes by moving them back into their heads. This leaves the shark blind, or unable to see! Instead, sharks use their electrical senses to know when it's time to bite.

# Different Dinners

Sharks eat different foods depending on where they live and how big they are. Most sharks eat only meat. They usually eat fish, squids, lobsters, and crabs. Some will even eat other sharks! Sharks such as bonnetheads will also eat seagrass.

## Finding Their Way

Sharks also use their electrical senses to find their way through the ocean. A shark uses its receptors to follow Earth's **magnetic field**. The shark uses it to find their way home or find their way to warmer or cooler water!

# GLOSSARY

**electricity:** A kind of energy that flows and is made by the movements of animals.

**electric field:** An area of force surrounding a body with electrical charge.

**evolve:** To grow and change over time.

**jaws:** The bones that hold the teeth and make up the mouth.

**magnetic field:** The area around Earth where magnetic forces can be found.

**muscle:** One of the parts of the body that allow movement.

**protect:** To keep safe.

**receptors:** Part of an animal's body that senses changes in its surroundings, like hot or cold.

**scale:** One of the flat plates that cover an animal's body.

**sensitive:** Able to sense or feel changes in surroundings.

# FOR MORE INFORMATION

## BOOKS

Kim, Carol. *Shark Superpowers.* North Mankato, MN: Capstone Press: 2022.

Santos, Tracie. *Sharks and Other Fish.* Vero Beach, FL: Rourke Educational Media, 2021.

## WEBSITES

**Active Wild: Facts About Sharks**
*www.activewild.com/facts-about-sharks-for-kids/*
Find out more facts about the different kinds of sharks that live around the world.

**Sharks 4 Kids: Shark Senses**
*www.sharks4kids.com/shark-senses*
Learn more about a shark's senses and how they find food in the wild.

# INDEX